MW00424295

# The SILENT Pandemic After COVID-19

## What You Won't Notice and Your Children Can't Tell You

### Diana F Cameron

**KIDS** DISC VER

Kids Discover Publishing

# Copyright

I dedicate this book to all children who are struggling in the aftermath of COVID-19 and to my 2 grandchildren that I have not been able to see because of the pandemic.

# Disclaimer

I f you are suffering severely from anxiety, depression, or fear, please seek medical advice. The information contained within is intended to give you strategies to use at home (or in the classroom) to help children navigate the aftereffects of COVID-19. It is not intended to replace medical advice. It is intended as educational information only.

To the maximum extent permitted by law, the author makes no statement, representation, or warranty about the quality, accuracy, context, completeness, or suitability for any purpose of any material available in this book. The author disclaims, to the maximum extent permitted by law, all responsibility, and all liability (including without limitation, liability in negligence) for all expenses, losses, damages and costs you or any other person might incur for any reason because of the information available in this book being in any way inaccurate, out of context, incomplete, not up to date or unsuitable for any purpose.

# Contents

# Counting the Cost of COVID-19

How has COVID-19 impacted your life? Maybe you or your partner lost a job? Maybe you were self-employed, and the shutdowns will take you years to recover from? Maybe you had to completely close your business, dealing with the stress of having to let staff go and losing the only livelihood you had?

Maybe you or your partner had to home-school children, thinking at first that it would just be a month or two but having it extend longer and longer. Before too long, a year had passed, and you wondered if there was ever going to be an end in sight.

Maybe, like me, it prevented you from seeing family and loved ones, and you were isolated? Maybe you had COVID yourself or a loved one had it and you had the stress of having to care for them. Maybe it was worse, and you lost a loved one, or more than just one.

Maybe the constant mask wearing, and hand sanitizing has been stressful to you. Maybe you have respiratory issues and mask wearing has been even more of a challenge.

The cost of COVID and the impact of shutdowns and isolation, mask wearing, hand sanitizing and constantly changing rules has been stressful for everyone. Do you really know the full impact of the pandemic on you personally? Have you sat down and really taken stock of what it has amounted to in your life, on your health, your mental state, or your financial situation?

Maybe it hasn't ended and the stress of the decision to vaccinate or not has plagued you. Maybe employment has been impacted even now that things have begun to open up again because of that decision if you chose not to vaccinate? The pandemic has been difficult for all of us. Even if you got to keep your job, the added stress of a totally foreign and unpredictable lifestyle has been overwhelming.

I don't know that we will fully understand the toll it has taken for many years.

But what of our children? Have you thought about the impact this has had and is having on them?

Try to think about it from a small child's perspective. The entire world changed overnight. They could no longer go outside to play. They were confined, restricted (which never works long term for young children), unable to express what they were feeling because they either had no clue (because this was unfamiliar territory) or they were too little and didn't have the cognitive processes to be able to express those feelings.

My granddaughter was 22 months old when COVID-19 hit. The last time I saw her was when she was 10 months old. We used to joke at the beginning (having no idea of the true seriousness or how long this would last) that she would be in school before I saw her again. With the borders in Australia only just starting to open (and slowly), the reality is she will indeed be in full time school by the time I get to see her again.

At 3 ½ years, she has spent half of the most formative years of her life inside, without social interaction, without the physical nature of playing outside a 2-bedroom apartment. She lives in the United States in a cold climate which means her winters are already more restricted in comparison with my climate (I live in Queensland Australia). To have no outside time in addition to the stresses that COVID brought, there is no denying it has all had an impact. She has lived her life inside an apartment, living amongst stressors that she and her parents were not aware of.

Being confined inside subjects us to invisible toxins (which we will explore in chapter 8) that you won't even be aware of that impact your life in every way, making it harder to cope, harder to relax and more stressful than the pandemic that is going on outside. We will talk later about this toxic stress situation and how you can minimize these stressors in your children's lives with easy strategies you can use at home.

Being inside 24/7 denies children normal routines where child development skills are practiced, and milestones reached.

I believe there is a pandemic after COVID-19. It is a silent pandemic amongst our children.

In both my professional and personal life, I am now seeing more anxiety and fear in children than ever before. I don't believe we have seen the full effects on child development and emergent skills, and I think in the unfolding years ahead these will become more evident.

My hope is that the information in this book will help you to be aware, identify and acknowledge the cost to yourself and your children, and provide you with strategies to help guide them back to a place of calm and well-being.

Before we can do any of that, we need to really acknowledge and pinpoint what that cost has been. It will be different for each of us, depending on our circumstances, our personalities, pre-existing conditions, and our age.

You will see later how young children are handcuffed in navigating this new post-COVID world because of the child developmental stage they are at. Adolescents also have challenges as brains are not fully developed until they are 25 years old.

So first, take time to make a list. This may take you more than an hour. It may even require several days of thinking but the more accurate you are at pinpointing the cost for you and your children, the easier it is to see where the challenges are and to implement strategies to support them.

I want you to make a list for every person in your household. Just because you are both parents, living in the same household, your experiences will have been different and the cost to you personally will be different from your partners. The same goes for each of your children. Personality, prior experience, resilience, skills, and knowledge will all play a part in determining what the individual cost is for each person.

There are two things I want you to think about: the obvious cost and the not so obvious. This will take some time, so think about this over the next little while or even take a couple of days to really identify what COVID-19 has cost you personally. Really think deeper than the surface and think of every way COVID has impacted you and your children (individually).

Here are some points to think about that may help you identify some of these costs. There will be many more than

I have mentioned here but this should start the thought process.

## PARENTS/ADULTS
### Obvious Factors:

- Job/employment loss
- Employment hours cut (so financial cost)
- Business that had to close completely
- Staff that had to be let go
- Loss of loved ones
- Physical cost (you may have had COVID or cared for someone who did)
- Emotional costs – feeling fearful not knowing how to keep your children safe or if they would get it

### Not So Obvious Factors:

- Social Gatherings: with restrictions, we could no longer go for a drink with friends, visit people for a movie night or do any of the normal social things we usually have in our routine. Relaxation time is missed. Couple that with all the added stress and the cost is great - you are in high alert all the time.

- Confined indoors: you might be a physical person who loves the outdoors. To be deprived of exercise routines or just walking outside is a cost that is not so obvious.

- Self Esteem: You may feel less confident now, less motivated to do things

- Time lost learning new technology and skills because you had to change to working from home

- Upgrades you may have had to make to work from home

- Lost time with loved ones outside the home

- Quality time with kids may have suffered because you were all in a stressful fishbowl for too long

- Relationship with your significant other may have been put to the test

## WHAT IS THE COST FOR YOUR CHILDREN?
**Obvious Factors:**

- Loss of routine

- Loss of activities (swimming, sports, group music sessions etc)

- Having to home-school (schoolwork not as easy online, loss of daily contact with friends)

- Feelings of isolation being stuck inside

**Not So Obvious Factors:**

- Poor sleep due to nightmares

- Feeling anxious all the time

- Mood changes

- Personality changes

- Not able to control emotions (like they are on an emotional roller coaster)

- Fearful of parents dying from COVID

- Fearful of themselves getting COVID

- Fearful that any "virus" will kill their parents or themselves

- School grades dropped

- Loss of confidence in themselves

- Loss of time - learning new ways of doing things, schoolwork, organization etc

- Loss of connection – how they view themselves as connected to others in family and people outside the family

- Decreased ability to focus

# Children Have Limited Understanding

We know from previous child development information that children's brains are not capable of processing things in the same way as adults. Children are sensory creatures, and their brains develop from the bottom up.

That means there is a highly organized way in which the brain interprets information and how children acquire skills.

Let's look at the pyramid of learning. As you can see, the foundation of the pyramid houses all our sensory systems. Children interpret the world through their senses. When they are born, these senses are underdeveloped, and they have primitive reflexes that help them navigate the world.

Gradually, these primitive reflexes are integrated and replaced with higher level learning. Jerky, primitive movements become smoother, and the brain is better able to comprehend more difficult concepts.

If the development of these sensory systems is compromised, then that affects learning that comes in the more advanced sections of the pyramid.

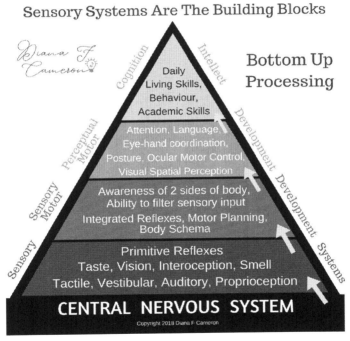

*Sensory Systems: The Building Blocks*

Our eight sensory systems make up the foundation and support all higher learning. Later you will see how COVID-19 and our resultant circumstances have interrupted the normal progression of more than one of these systems.

Jean Piaget (a Swiss psychologist) was the first to make a systematic study on how children acquire skills. His work forms the basis for many currently held child development theories.

Piaget named several stages of development for children. These were:

- Sensorimotor stage: birth to 2 years
- Preoperational stage: ages 2 to 7
- Concrete operational stage: ages 7 to 11
- Formal operational stage: ages twelve and up

The formal operational stage (from 11 or 12 years) is when tweens are starting to be able to understand abstract ideas. In the early stages, for example preschoolers, they are unable to understand an idea like 1+1=2.

This is an abstract idea that has no meaning to them. The brain is unable to process the information and relate it to anything. For them to understand, they need to use their senses. They need to hear, feel, see, touch – the more senses they can use, the easier and deeper the learning will be.

If you give a 4-year-old one apple, and ask them how many that is, they will be able to tell you it is 1 apple. Then if you brought out another apple, they would be able to count 1, 2 for each of the apples and work out there are 2 apples in total. This works because they have something concrete to hold and see.

Once children start going to school, you may see some of them still struggling with concepts of math. It could be that the brain has not acquired the concepts they need to understand yet. If you have a switched-on teacher, they will use "rods" or other tactile objects to teach these concepts because it just makes sense to the child.

If there are sensory issues, these can sometimes stop those types of concepts sticking in the brain and they just won't retain the information.

So, children up to tweens don't have the cognitive capability to understand what a pandemic is – it is an abstract idea. It isn't something they can see, touch or hear. They can't comprehend what it is, why their routines have suddenly changed and why everyone is so stressed. Without being able to process complex information, the massive changes in their lives must be incredibly overwhelming.

One study done in September 2020 by five lecturers all from the department of psychology in the University of Bath, UK (Haig-Ferguson, A. et al [1]) stated "This makes it more difficult for children to understand abstract information, such as a 'viral' health-related threat. Their emergent beliefs are also more malleable than those of adults and are influenced and shaped by significant others."

Children's emergent beliefs are influenced by your reactions and conversations as their parents. Unable to understand it themselves, all they can do is formulate those ideas and beliefs from what they see, hear, and feel around them.

That doesn't mean we can't change those beliefs or replace them with more positive, reassuring ones that will help support them but if all they have heard is fearful conversations, television reports of death tolls and fear mongering in the media, that is where they are going to form their views on what is happening.

1. Haig-Ferguson, A., Cooper, K., Cartwright, E., Loades, M., & Daniels, J. (2021). Practitioner review: Health anxiety in children and young people in the context of the COVID-19 pandemic. Behavioural and Cognitive Psychotherapy, 49(2), 129-143. doi:10.1017/S1352465820000636

# Psychological and Neurobiological Effects

The instances of anxiety and depression in our children have far exceeded estimates prior to the pandemic, in fact, they have doubled.

A study done in August 2021 by Sheri Madigan et al [1], stated that "in addition to a near doubling in clinically elevated depressive and anxiety symptoms in children and adolescents during the COVID-19 pandemic, there have been increases in other mental health concerns, including eating disorders (EDs)."

The National Child Traumatic Stress Network (2020) [2] stated the psychological responses to COVID-19 will change with age as follows:

**PRESCHOOL**

- Manifestations of fear

- Loss of appetite
- Increased tantrums and complaints
- Ambivalent anxiety

**6 – 12 YEARS**

- higher rates of irritability
- nightmares
- sleep problems
- appetite problems
- somatic symptoms
- loss of interest in peers
- excessive attachment to parents

**13 – 18 YEARS**

In addition to the physical problems:

- sleep problems
- isolation
- increased or decreased energy
- higher rates of apathy
- inattention to behaviors related to health care

In an extensive study [3] done in February 2021 through the Universities of Malaga and Alicante on the effects of COVID-19 on Spanish children, they found the part of society that was extremely susceptible to isolation was the "child and adolescent population since the contexts in which they live and develop are altered."

It's findings further supported the National Child Traumatic Stress Network's statements when it said that emotional stress had neurobiological consequences (so brain and body) such as increased rates of anxiety, depression, sleep disorders and acute stress.

Restorative sleep occurs because of a dynamic biopsychosocial balance – a delicate balance between biological (body), psychological (mind), and social conditions. A balance between all three is needed for restorative sleep to occur.

With added stress, anxiety, fear, and depression impacting on that balance, we end up with sleep disorders, or a disruption of that restorative sleep. This leaves our sleep experience inadequate to allow our central nervous system to disengage and relax and our bodies to restore adequately.

The Spanish study further explained that with these emotional and sleep problems, it was not unreasonable to think that cognitive processes can be affected in situations of confinement.

We all know what it is like when we don't get sleep and we are stressed. We can't think straight and our performance at any task is subpar.

The study further clarified that it has been observed that stress (both acute and chronic) affects cognitive processes governed by the Prefrontal Cortex. We have certainly been exposed to acute stress with the effects of COVID-19 and it has gone on long enough for it to become chronic in nature.

To understand this more fully, we need to be aware of what processes the Prefrontal Cortex of the brain is responsible for. Then we will have a better understanding of issues our children may be dealing with,

## The Prefrontal Cortex is responsible for the processes and functions of the executive system.

- Working memory
- Self-regulation of emotions
- Cognitive flexibility
- Organization and planning
- Decision making
- Goal orientated behaviors
- Inhibitory Control

**Because of the effects of COVID-19, our children may have trouble with:**

- Remembering things
- Keeping their emotions in check. Something small may happen and they might meltdown. The response will not match the situation
- Social situations

• Stopping what they want to do and doing another task that you may want them to do

• Understanding things. Cognitive flexibility is the ability to switch between two different concepts or to think about multiple concepts simultaneously.

• Organizing themselves or their thoughts

• Solving problems

• Planning

• Making decisions

• Having a desire to reach goals or to move forward – they will have general apathy

## COGNITIVE FLEXIBILITY

Cognitive flexibility affects things that you may not realize. It is what is needed to understand that Mom has gone out of the room and will return later. Children need to manage two sets of data for this task:

1. Where is Mom? Is she ok?

2. How do I feel about Mom leaving? Am I ok?

Children with autism normally struggle with this skill because their minds tend to focus on single items or sets of data. For some things, the child with autism might understand but for others that you may think are the same they don't. For example: A child with autism can understand that their drink bottle is in the bag racks outside the classroom. They will understand that concept because they are dealing with one set of data. The bottle is in the bag.

The same child with autism might meltdown when Mom leaves the room. This requires the two sets of data mentioned above. They need the sense of interoception to acquire this skill because interoception allows them to read what is happening inside their body (one set of data – how do I feel about Mom leaving) as well as what is happening outside their body (data set number 2 – where is Mom? Is she ok? Will she come back?)

To process these two sets of data simultaneously needs the processes of the prefrontal cortex and cognitive flexibility. Can you imagine during COVID conditions having this suppressed? Is it any wonder that children become clingier and more anxious? It goes much deeper than just feeling unsure or being needy. Are you starting to see the effects are much more than just making them anxious because of the change in our circumstances?

Multiple studies prior to COVID have linked the role of these functions as mediators between perceived stress and memory complaints. For a lot of children and adolescents, there is a lot of perceived stress associated with the pandemic.

- Will my family be ok?
- Will my parents die?
- What will happen to me if they do?
- Will my parents get sick?
- Will I get sick?

- Will I ever get to be with my friends again?

Perceived stress is very real and even though they may not have lived in a heavily affected area, it doesn't mean their perceived stress wasn't high. The effects on body and brain from perceived stress are the same as actual stress. The brain sees all stress as a threat and takes measures to protect itself and the body. This means symptoms that we have discussed previously.

Sprang and Silman [4] did a study in 2013 that found children who had been quarantined during pandemics were more likely to develop acute stress disorders, adjustment disorders and physical pain.

In a Chinese study [5] of children 3 – 18 years in the Shaanxi Province in China during COVID-19, they found that 30% of all children studied in isolation or quarantine met the clinical criteria for post-traumatic stress disorder (PTSD).

This same study also showed that children aged 3 to 6 years were more likely than older children to manifest symptoms such as anxiety and fear that family members could become infected. Children 6 to 18 were more likely to show inattention and persistent inquiry.

Common amongst all children was inattention and irritability and the population where the most severe psychological conditions were demonstrated.

1. Racine N, Vaillancourt T, Madigan S. Effect of the COVID-19 Pandemic on Adolescents with Eating Disorders—Reply. JAMA Pediatr. Published online November 15, 2021. doi:10.1001/jamapediatrics.2021.4681

2. National Child Traumatic Stress Network (2020). Guía de Ayuda Para Padres y Cuidadores Para Ayudar a las Familias a Enfrentar la Enfermedad Coronavirus 2019 (COVID-19). Los Angeles, CA: National Child Traumatic Stress Network.

3. Lavigne-Cerván R, Costa-López B, Juárez-Ruiz de Mier R, Real-Fernández M, Sánchez-Muñoz de León M and Navarro-Soria I (2021) Consequences of COVID-19 Confinement on Anxiety, Sleep and Executive Functions of Children and Adolescents in Spain. Front. Psychol. 12:565516. doi: 10.3389/fpsyg.2021.565516

4. Sprang, G., and Silman, M. (2013). Posttraumatic stress disorder in parents and youth after health-related disasters. Disaster Med. Public Health Prepared. 7, 105–110. doi: 10.1017/dmp.2013.22

5. Ji, L. N., Chao, S., Wang, Y. J., Li, X. J., Mu, X. D., Lin, M. G., et al. (2020). Clinical features of pediatric patients with COVID-19: a report of two family cluster cases. World J. Pediatr. 16, 267–270. doi: 10.1007/s12519-020-00356-2

# The Prefrontal Cortex and Behavior

W ith the prefrontal cortex impacting the executive system, we are going to see changes in behavior when these systems are not working correctly. You may have noticed that your child used to adapt to change more easily than they do now.

Executive function and self-regulation are responsible for how a child responds to change.

Executive functions enable us to work effectively with others in a social setting, to keep on task even though distractions are all around us and to complete tasks with multiple demands simultaneously.

Research[1] has found that toxic stress (like we have seen because of COVID) can derail executive function. This research has also proven that children who experience intense, ongoing stress (which we have during COVID - toxic stress) tend to have lower executive function capabilities and are at a higher risk for physical and mental health problems.

> *"We can't ignore that biological and neurological changes have occurred over that time, (COVID-19) and we are now seeing behaviors associated with diminished skills."*
> Diana F Cameron

**From a behavioral standpoint, executive function enables us to:**

- make plans
- anticipate things
- respond to the consequences of our own actions
- multitask in an effective manner
- be patient with others

Poor executive function means we will struggle with these things and that impacts directly on behavior.

Think about something like taking turns. Say you are playing a board game together. Your child needs to be able to stop their turn to enable the next person to take theirs (Inhibitory control).

While the next person is taking their turn, they then must remember what they will need to do when it is their turn again (working memory).

Then they need to respond to what the other turn takers have done when their turn comes around again. If others have done something unpredictable or different to what they thought they would do, they may then need to change their response during their turn so that play continues (cognitive flexibility).

This simple act of playing a board game together (and subsequent turn taking) requires a variety of executive function skills. They are the foundation for social, academic, and emotional success.

You see this in action when a child is playing a board game or taking turns, if the other person doesn't do what they think they should have done, or the game doesn't follow what they had predicted in their minds, they can't cope and get frustrated, which leads quickly to anger and throwing the items across the room (no emotional regulation). That is the result of a poorly functioning prefrontal cortex and subsequent executive functions.

I am commonly hearing these types of comments from parents about their children:

> "They used to be engaged and love learning but now they don't even want to do the things they used to love"

> "I ask them to do simple things and they can't seem to figure it out. They just stare at me."

"They take forever to do mundane tasks like getting dressed."

"They lose their patience with siblings much faster than they used to."

"They lose it over the smallest thing. They seem to have a really short fuse."

"My kids used to love playing together but now they are at each other all the time. I feel like I live my life being a referee."

"They seem exhausted all the time."

"They don't have any attention span at all."

You can see how these things relate to executive function being compromised. Much of it we might have put down to just being inside all the time, or in close quarters with their siblings.

While I am sure that was also a contributing factor, we can't ignore that biological and neurological changes have occurred over time, and we are now seeing behaviors associated with diminished skills.

## ACTIVITIES TO HELP TEACH EXECUTIVE FUNCTION

Executive function and self-regulation skills appear very early in the development of a child and are refined through practice through adolescence and into their 20s. Conversely, children who have endured toxic stress in these early years will struggle to develop these skills.

If your child is struggling with the behaviors we have spoken about, work with some of these activities to provide opportunities to practice these skills.

## INHIBITORY CONTROL

Inhibitory control (which is just another name for impulse control) is a foundational skill as part of the executive skills which is the child being able to stop what they are doing (what they want to do) and attend to another task. It goes along with anticipation, which is a skill that this generation is sadly lacking.

We live in a world of instant gratification. We no longer save up for things, we pay with afterpay. We don't wait for our weekly episode of our favorite TV program; we binge on Netflix. Everything in our society is about getting it right away and it has not done our children any favors.

## ANTICIPATION FIRST

We need to build the skill of anticipation before we build the higher cognitive skill of inhibitory control. We can do this from the time our children are born with simple and fun games.

The activities below will be familiar to you. We build anticipation by taking our time. Space in conversation is a way that our baby's brain is alerted that they need to pay attention. If there is counting involved leading to a reward like there is in these games, then take time getting there.

Use your facial expressions, your body language, and your voice to build that anticipation. Our voices usually become higher the closer we get to the reward (which is usually something like a tickle or a movement that is fun for baby).

**Ways to build anticipation might include:**

- Round and round the haystack

    Round and round the garden
    Goes the little bear
    One step...... Two steps......
    Tickley under there!

Here are a few extensions:

Round and round the beehive
Goes the little bee
One step...... Two steps......
Come and cuddle me!

Round and round the sleeping cat
Goes the little mouse
One step...... Two steps......
In his little house!

Round and round the stable
Goes the little horse
One step...... Two steps......
Gallop with me of course!

Round and round the robin
Circled in the sky
One flap...... Two flaps......
Swing way up high!

- Peekaboo games
- Hiding games

For children who lack inhibitory control, they will be the kids who can't sit next to someone without poking them or bothering them.

They will not be particularly good at turn-taking or controlling themselves in a quiet environment.

While it is possible to improve this skill, it takes time and repetition. Don't expect it to form all at once, even the slightest ability to stop on cue, even if only for one second before they take off again, should be celebrated. Then they can extend from there.

Just as with exercising the physical body, if we want to get stronger, we need to challenge the skill regularly, increasing the requirement from the game after a particular level of skill has been reached.

**Activities to help build inhibitory control are:**

• **Freezing games:** This is usually a staple with children and something children love. Some children will be able to freeze the minute you say "freeze" or stop the music, but others will keep going no matter what you do. They lack the ability to "stop on cue" and control those impulses that tell them to keep going. Repeating games like this over and over where they must freeze on cue allows them the opportunity to practice this skill. It is only through repetition that the skill is acquired. A variation would be to stand like a statue in a different pose every time. Extend the time of stopping a little each time which also builds the ability to resist impulses and control the body. Making the rule that they must walk or dance, not run during the musical segments, will add another layer of complexity for those struggling with this skill.

- **Balloon Volleyball:** Hitting a balloon in the air over a net to another team without having it touch the ground. Teams can count how many times they can do it before it hits the floor. This helps because they need to control the impulse to hit the balloon too hard, or it will not be able to be controlled as easily and will end up on the floor.

- **Hide and Seek:** Someone waits and counts while others hide after which they find them. This encourages the child to wait while they are being found. You see this in young children who do not have this skill where they will hide and then tell you where they are or just come out right away. There is no ability to wait until they are found.

- **Simon Says:** We all know how this one goes. One person gets to be "Simon" and calls out instructions. Children follow ONLY when Simon says. If an instruction is given without the prefacing "Simon says" they shouldn't move. This helps children to fight the impulse to perform the action when the words "Simon says" are not said.

- **Cooking Together:** Cooking together is a great way to help practice this skill. Children have to wait for you to tell them what to do, they have to wait to see what the finished product is going to be and wait before they can eat it. If your child really struggles with this skill use a really simple recipe with few ingredients and few steps. Progress to more complicated recipes as your child is able to wait a little longer. The longer and more complicated the recipe, the more inhibitory control and patience that is needed.

- **Games:** Anything requiring turn taking will help to develop inhibitory control. Whether it is sports or board games, they all provide opportunities to practice the skill over and over.

**Other Activities to Help with Executive Function:**

**ACTIVITIES      THAT      IMPROVE WORKING MEMORY:**

- Matching games
- Concentration
- Singing rounds

**ACTIVITIES      THAT      IMPROVE ATTENTION:**

- Duck duck goose
- Musical chairs
- Reading books like I Spy
- Learning a musical instrument
- Dance
- Yoga
- Martial Arts
- Sports

**ACTIVITIES      THAT      PROMOTE PLANNING AND PROBLEM SOLVING:**

- Brain Teaser Puzzles

- Scavenger Hunts made from a series of clues
- Crossword Puzzles
- Puzzles (age appropriate)

Improving executive function is going to show in behavior with children who will have increased social skills (and patience in peer driven situations), better focus and attention span and great control over their own bodies.

That control will not only extend to the physical body, but to their emotional self, giving them a much greater command over their responses to everyday situations.

1. Gormley Jr., W. T., Phillips, D. A., Newmark, K., Welti, K. and Adelstein, S. Gormley Jr., W. et al. (2011) "Social-Emotional Effects of Early Childhood Education Programs in Tulsa", Child Development, 82(6), pp. 2095-2109. doi: 10.1111/j.1467-8624.2011.01648.x.

# The Triad of Learning – Auditory

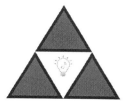 

L et's look at what I call the Triad of Learning. The triad has three main systems that collide with and are held together with our sensory system. These systems do not work independently of each other and while most are responsible for certain tasks, other systems play a part in how they operate.

We have all heard of the term "multi-sensory learning". This is how children learn best because all these systems are emerging and how young children interpret the world around them. Each of these systems are essential, and while one system can become heightened in the total absence of another (for example if a child is born without sight, their auditory system will be much more acute), if there are skills not acquired or missing from one or more system, there will be deficits in learning.

Another example is a child that is born without hearing, or compromised hearing. While technology has come a long way in cochlea implants, speech is always challenged when the auditory system is down.

We have twelve essential auditory skills and when one or more has not developed, we see skills that are compromised.

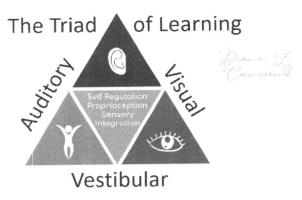

*The Triad of Learning*

**The three main systems are:**

- Auditory
- Visual and
- Vestibular

As we saw in diagram one, our brains build from the bottom up and all these systems are at the foundational level.

As we learn more about one of these systems, auditory, and what it is primarily responsible for, I want you to think about them in the context not only of general child development, but specifically in relation to the conditions we have endured for 18 months.

Many children, like my grandson, will have been born into a pandemic environment with restricted conditions. It will be all they know.

When you understand the importance of these systems and how they normally develop, you will see that intervention is now needed to not only help our children psychologically to deal with stress, but to acquire skills that would normally develop during childhood play.

For many children, because of living conditions, all play has been in extremely confined spaces. It may have been an apartment, townhouse, dwelling where extended families also live as well as their immediate family.

Inside doesn't just have size restrictions but also noise limitations, something that is challenging for children long-term.

## ALFRED TOMATIS: REVOLUTIONARY FOR HIS TIME

Alfred Tomatis was a French ear, nose and throat specialist who was born in 1920. His research was revolutionary and still serves as the basis for sound therapy today.

In his book, The Power of Sound" [1] Joshua Leeds states the six key principles of how sound affects the body. These six things were:

1. The ear is like a battery with a primary function of converting sound waves to electrical waves that charge the cortex of the brain.

2. Sound is a nutrient; we can either charge or discharge the nervous system by the sounds we take in through both air and bone conduction

3. There is a distinction between hearing and listening. These two auditory functions are related but distinct. Hearing is passive, listening is active and conscious. On a visual level, this corresponds to the difference between seeing and looking. Listening and looking are active focusing processes.

4. The quality of an individual's listening ability will affect not only spoken and written language development but also alertness, creativity, and the ability to focus. Listening abilities also influence communication thereby shaping social development, confidence, and self-image.

5. Communication is a process that begins in utero. The unborn child hears as early as the fourth month after conception. Sound literally helps the brain and the nervous system of the fetus to grow.

6. The voice can only reproduce what the ear hears. We can only duplicate the sounds that we can hear. This is known as the Tomatis Effect.

I want to concentrate on just a few of them. Let's look at number 2. "Sound is a nutrient; we can either charge or discharge the nervous system by the sounds we take in through both air and bone conduction."

One thing Tomatis used to say is that the body is a giant ear. We don't just process sound through our ears (air conduction) but also our skeletal system (bone conduction). When I work with a client with sound therapy, we use headphones that go across the head. In this band there is a sensor at the top of the skull. This allows sound to be produced and processed by bone conduction as well as air conduction. The two together are much gentler and the gains we see are greater in a shorter period. You can even safely continue listening if you have an ear infection by turning off the air conduction component and just listen with bone conduction.

It is a fascinating experience. The first time I listened with just the bone conduction sensor activated, I could hear every instrument in the orchestra. It was muffled like you were underwater, but all the sounds were there. I was astounded and it reiterated to me the amount of work our body and ears must do 24/7 in processing sounds that come at us in our environment.

That is why our voice sounds different when we hear a recording of it. When we speak it resonates through our skull (bone) and our ears, so we hear it with both. When recorded, we experience an air conduction version of it (which we usually find very unappealing).

It is a system that we can't shut off, it is working all the time, even when we sleep. There is a saying in the sound therapy world "We don't have earlids." Think about our visual system. We shut our eyes we give it a rest, but with our auditory system, we can't do that.

We can hear through walls and around corners. Even if we put on noise cancelling headphones, our body is still processing. Have you ever seen a hearing-impaired person dance to the beat of music? Or put their feet on a speaker and clap to the beat? They are processing sound through their skeletal system.

Once the sounds come in through these two avenues (body and ears) they are then transformed into electrochemical signals and sent to the various auditory pathways to the brain.

For children and adults with poor auditory processing skills, this can be exhausting. Children with autism have auditory processing challenges. I have not worked with one in the past 25 years that didn't. It just seems to go with the territory.

Children on the spectrum also have poor filtration systems to filter out unwanted noise. Your children are the same and babies' filters are the most fragile yet. The more listening and processing we do, the better our auditory skills. So, children on the spectrum, those with ADHD, young children and babies may already have struggles in this area. Add a COVID environment and we have just expounded the challenges.

Tomatis also discovered that depending on the pitch (Hz) of the sound, it had a different effect on the body. Advanced Brain Technologies[2] base their sound therapy (of which I am a certified practitioner) around these three zones which are:

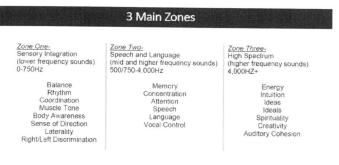

*Three Main Zones of Listening*

Let's look at them and what skills are associated with them.

# ZONE ONE

*Zone One: Sensory Integration (Skills that relate to good processing in this zone)*

This zone includes all the low frequency tones. These affect our bodies, self-regulation, body awareness, coordination, and timing. Not processing tones in this range causes problems because it is the foundational level for all higher functions.

**<u>Poor processing</u> of these pitches will result in some or many of the following being difficult:**

- Being able to relax
- Reducing your stress
- Balance
- Sense of rhythm

- Coordination
- Muscle tone
- Body awareness
- Sense of direction
- Laterality
- Right and left discrimination
- Tantrums and meltdowns will be longer
- The frequency of tantrums and meltdowns will be more
- Poor sleep

Low level tones are the basses, cellos, certain timpani, and tubas of an orchestra. Naturally occurring sounds in this range would be things like:

- Large dogs barking
- Lawnmowers
- The sound of thunder
- Earthquakes
- Whales
- Elephants
- Waves crashing on the beach
- Men's voices

A note to make is that processing sound is quite different to hearing. You can have a perfect audiogram and still not process sounds well. We will look at what needs to happen for good processing in the next chapter.

## ZONE TWO

Zone Two contains mid and upper-level frequencies, including our speech and language, most of which sits between 3,000 – 4,000Hz.

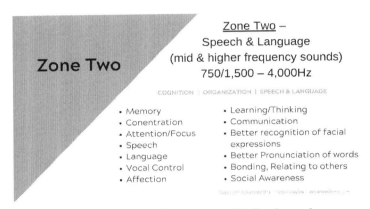

Zone Two –
Speech & Language
(mid & higher frequency sounds)
750/1,500 – 4,000Hz

COGNITION | ORGANIZATION | SPEECH & LANGUAGE

- Memory
- Conentration
- Attention/Focus
- Speech
- Language
- Vocal Control
- Affection

- Learning/Thinking
- Communication
- Better recognition of facial expressions
- Better Pronunciation of words
- Bonding, Relating to others
- Social Awareness

*Zone Two: Speech and Language (Skills that relate to good processing in this zone)*

**If you are having issues with processing sounds in zone two then you might have difficulty with one or more of the following:**

- Processing higher voices like young girls or women

- Beginnings or endings of words. You might swap out sounds like "free" for "three".

- Rhyming words - hearing the similarities and differences of sounds

• Forming certain consonants or vowel sounds correctly (speech may be hard to understand because the child is producing what the brain is "hearing" but because processing is not accurate, it comes out differently than what you hear, or how you pronounce words

• Chinese whispers or interpreting what someone has whispered in your ear

Mid to higher level tones are the flutes, piccolos and violins of an orchestra. Naturally occurring sounds in this range would be things like:

• Birdsong

• Someone whispering in your ear

• Babbling streams as the water goes over rocks

• Rainfall on your umbrella

• Dogs whining

• Collar tags jingling

• A child squealing

• Crackling of pine needles as you go on a walk

• Leaves rustling in the wind – Scientists have found that "Needle-like leaves, or petioles, shed vortices as the wind oscillates round them, creating the high-pitched, romantic whisper of conifers."[3]

## ZONE THREE

There is a third listening zone that is responsible for our creativity and motivation.

The sounds in this zone are the highest we can audibly hear. They inspire us, get us moving and motivated. These are the highest frequencies ranging from 5,000 - 20,000Hz. We can audibly hear frequencies from 0 – 20,000Hz.

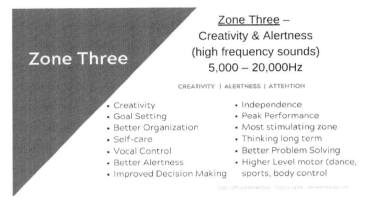

*Zone Three: Creativity & Alertness*

Processing tones in this zone effectively will give us the following advantages:

- Creativity

- Goal setting

- Better organization

- More self-care

- Better vocal control

- Better alertness

- Improved decision making

- Greater independence

- Help us reach peak performance

- It is the most stimulating zone we have (in a positive way)

- Thinking long term

- Better problem solving

- Higher level motor (dance, sports, body control for example for fast body movements

- Be more responsible

- More willing to act

- More future thinking (beyond here and now)

- Less need for reminding, prompting and instructions

- Thinking beyond the moment and realizing actions have consequences. The decisions you make now have consequences in the future.

- More willing to keep going with tasks and less likely to quit

As we age, these are the sounds that go first. There is a great website that gives demonstrations of sounds from 8,000 Hz and above. It details ages where processing and hearing certain sounds start to degenerate and then gives a recorded example of what a sound at that pitch (Hz) sounds like. You will find that here: https://decibelhearing.com/high-frequency-hearing-loss/

1. Leeds, J., 2010. The Power of Sound. Rochester: Inner Traditions International, Limited.

2.  Advanced Brain Technologies | www.advancedbrain.com

3. https://www.newscientist.com/lastword/mg20727672-800-whispering-trees/

# The Brain Needs Variety

We need variety in our listening environment. Remember Tomatis and his discovery that sound is a nutrient – it can either charge or discharge our central nervous system.

Our brain naturally attends to new things. When we experience something new, it sends out the beginnings of new connections (neural wiring). With repetition over time, those connections become strong.

If we don't have enough repetition, or if we no longer use that skill after a period, the brain is efficient and prunes the connections that are no longer being used to make room for new ones.

Imagine if we only ate one thing, day in and day out for months or years. We would become extremely ill because our body needs a variety of vitamins, minerals, and other nutrients to facilitate the many processes that allow us to function in a normal way.

Even eliminating one thing can cause issues. When people don't get enough vitamin C, they end up with the following possible symptoms:

- Feeling very tired and weak all the time
- feeling irritable and sad all the time
- have severe joint or leg pain
- have swollen, bleeding gums (sometimes teeth can fall out)
- develop red or blue spots on the skin, usually on your shins
- have skin that bruises easily

Scurvy is the deficiency of one element of all the nutrients we need and yet it can have devastating effects on the body as a whole.

The same happens with our auditory system. When we are deprived of the opportunity of processing certain sounds, it can affect an array of skills, some of which you would not even associate with not being able to process sounds correctly.

> *"Just as our physical body needs a variety of nutrients to remain healthy and strong, we need a variety of sounds in our auditory diet to help our brain be better organized."*
> Diana F Cameron

The auditory system works with the brain to know what we are hearing. It is known as auditory processing. It is what our brain does with what we hear. In a simplified sense, sound comes in through the ears and skeletal system, it goes to the brain via the eighth cranial nerve, and the brain identifies, interprets, and catalogs those sounds, comparing them to previous experience and formulates a response based on previous knowledge.

That is an over simplified description and there is a lot that happens on the way, but if the brain has not had enough practice at interpreting sounds, then areas of learning can be affected as we saw in our listening zones and what skills they are connected to.

We not only need practice processing those sounds but we need a wide range of sounds (and a balance across the spectrum) for those skills to be acquired.

For example, we have seen that low level sounds have to do with our bodies. These grounding sounds have to do with motor function, balance, body awareness etc. If we only heard low level sounds, we would not have speech. We would not be creative or motivated. We would be sluggish and slow because low level sounds discharge the central nervous system.

This can be an advantage when we want it to be. If we are trying to go to sleep, you would choose music with mostly low-level sounds rather than the higher, energetic sounds in zone three, which would charge our CNS.

If you are thinking "then why, when we have been stuck inside with all these low-level sounds are we more tired, more anxious and more depressed?" The key difference is patterns and no patterns which we will discuss in the next chapter.

Low level drones, or sound without patterns stress our central nervous system and makes us more anxious. Low level sounds with patterns discharge our CNS, allowing us to relax and be calm. It quietens the brain as opposed to making the brain work twice as hard as is the case with low level tones with no patterns (which we will name white noise).

There are a lot of variants in what people describe as white noise. White noise machines are sold with sounds of rain, or waves on the beach or static. Those sounds do not all have the same impact on our bodies and brains which we will look more deeply at in chapter 7.

Variety is the spice of life, so they say, but it certainly is necessary for a calm and well-organized brain. It is like a factory worker who does the same job day in and day out. The repetitiveness of his task does not inspire creativity. The brain shuts down and the actions become automatic, much like driving and other tasks we learn to do without actively thinking each step through.

To inspire creative thinking, those with repetitive work environments need to seek variety outside the work environment. Music can be a reliable source of both creating calm and inspiring creativity if the right music is chosen. Music is one activity that fires all areas of the brain and scientific studies done over the last 10 years have proven that.

It doesn't have to be music, there are other things that motivate the brain in addition to music.

**Some suggestions might be:**

- Learning to play an instrument
- Playing in a band or orchestra
- Singing in a choir
- Singing by yourself
- Listening to music (in fact, listening to music while doing repetitive tasks, if not dangerous, would help you be more productive and less fatigued. That is not practical for all work environments, but it may be for some).
- Sports
- Exercise
- Drawing or painting
- Doing sculpture
- Doing crosswords or sudoku

There are many things you could choose to do to stimulate the brain and help bring balance.

One thing to note is that video games do not bring that balance. It is overstimulating visually, the music is usually extremely poor quality and playing long hours of video games lessens the brain's ability to self-calm, think creatively and effects skills governed by the prefrontal cortex that we discussed earlier.

This is important for your children as well. Variety is needed for healthy brain function and a variety in auditory stimulation is key for the many different skills we looked at previously.

If we only heard low level sounds, we would have trouble with speech, if we only heard high-level sounds, we would have trouble with movement, coordination, body awareness, low muscle tone and all those other things in zone one.

In fact, we would have trouble with everything because zone one is the foundational zone. In working with a client with sound therapy, if there is a speech and language issue, I always lay the base with zone one sounds. If they are not processing those correctly, then zone two will be an issue as well.

This is achieved through specialized, psychoacoustically, modified music that uses filters to isolate the sounds we want to work with the most. For example, if we want to really work the brain, giving it experience and opportunity to process low level sounds, a high pass filter is used to take out a lot of the higher tones to make that possible. The reverse is true for mid and high tones.

Regardless of what activities and experiences you and your children choose, just remember that variety is key. Lots of experience listening to and learning to process different sounds will help the brain be more balanced and organized.

Think of the conditions we were living in during lockdowns and COVID-19 at its height. We were stuck inside with the hum of refrigerators, lights, microwaves, computers, air conditioners and heaters.

They are all low level tones which discharge our central nervous system, but we have been devoid of mid and higher-level sounds which aid speech and language development, creativity, goal setting, and motivation.

# The Brain is Built to Look for Patterns

We have all heard the phrase "music makes you smarter" but were you aware that music can help to quiet a disorganized brain?

So how is playing music beneficial and how can it help to calm the brain?

The rhythm and mathematical structure found within music gives the brain something to hang onto. The working memory part of the brain instinctively looks for patterns to combat fatigue and overwhelm that can happen with white noise that has no patterns. It is this structure and patterns that bring quiet to an overwhelmed and disorganized brain.

Music has many elements, the basic of which is beat or pulse. This primal language speaks to our brains and bodies as it is the first thing to develop in the womb – our pulse and heartbeat.

# RHYTHM IS PART OF WHO WE ARE

Pulse develops in a fetus usually between 21 – 28 days after conception, or 35 – 45 days after the last period. Even though the heart is not fully developed at that point (and won't be until a week 10), a heartbeat can be detected by a transvaginal ultrasound.

At this point, the heartbeat is extremely fast, around 160 – 180 beats per minute, later slowing to 110 – 160.

So steady beat/pulse is with us from the very beginning. This steady, unchanging beat is different to rhythm. It is steady and unchanging; it is primal and something everyone can feel at their very core. It is something the brain notices and our whole body can feel and attune to.

Rhythm is with us in many parts of our lives without us realizing it. People are innately musical, and we perform complex, rhythmic tasks everyday with ease.

**These include:**

- Walking
- Running
- Brushing our teeth
- Speech
- Playing sport
- Singing

Think about walking. We do it without thinking, and usually while talking (another complex task). Sometimes we even run and speak at the same time. Each of these individually is a complex progression of movements to a specific rhythm, and when we combine two actions with different rhythms flawlessly, that is a complex rhythmical accomplishment.

You will have a specific rhythm when brushing your teeth. You will do it the same way each day in a pattern and rhythm that you will not be consciously aware of. These rhythmic movements and others like swimming or biking are possible because of something called central pattern generators (CPGs). Simply put, CPGs are brain circuits that produce rhythmic outputs without being driven by external stimuli. We manage rhythmic patterns internally.

Rhythm is all around us and in us. It is a part of who we are. Our circadian rhythms are connected to the rhythm of the rising and setting of the sun. Heart attacks, strokes, high blood pressure, depression, cancer, insomnia, obesity, diabetes, dementia, migraines, and accidents all have been linked to disruptions in circadian rhythms.

The way a newborn breastfeeds is tied strongly to rhythm. In fact, when a newborn baby doesn't feed well, it is a sign to me that their internal rhythms may have been disrupted.

"People are innately musical, and we perform complex, rhythmic tasks everyday with ease."
Diana F Cameron

## WE RECOGNIZE RHYTHM & PITCH BEFORE WE ARE BORN

For a newborn, they have just come from a home that is filled with music. The rhythm of the mother's heartbeat, her breathing, the lyrical pitch and rhythm of her voice.

They arrive with immature auditory filters in place to a world with lots of sound, much of it white noise without rhythm such as air conditioners, traffic, fluorescent lights, and motors such as fridges, freezers, microwaves etc.

The brain is adept at recognizing and processing patterns, even complex patterns. According to research, newborns can tell the difference between their mother's voice and a voice that is not their mothers. There is even evidence [1] that a fetus prefers the mother's voice before they are born.

## MUSIC, PATTERNS AND THE BRAIN

Music is full of patterns. It gives the brain something to hang onto. We live in a world with many sounds without patterns and this type of white noise can be exhausting, particularly for babies and children. Music is filled with rhythm, steady beat, pitch patterns, rhythmic organization that the brain can recognize and relate to. With noise in our environment (such as white noise) which does not contain any of those properties, the brain is busy searching endlessly for patterns that do not exist. This leads to exhaustion and stress.

Think about long haul flights. The constant sound of the engine puts our brain into overdrive trying to find patterns in the sound. Even if you sleep, it doesn't stop as our auditory system cannot shut down. You get off the plane feeling exhausted, even if you have slept. Wearing noise cancelling headphones and playing music allows the brain to be in a more rested state than just sitting in the plane without intervention.

One of our twelve essential auditory skills that aids the brain in recognizing and utilizing these patterns in music is auditory memory. This skill enables us to seek out patterns and group things together which is less taxing on the brain and frees it up for other functions.

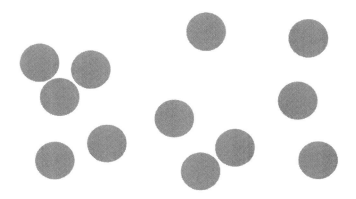

*Twelve Pieces of Incoming Information*

Imagine this diagram as information coming in through the ears and skeletal system. Think of it as music, with each dot representing a note or rhythm.

For our brains to process each sound individually it is time consuming and taxing as it works hard to decipher what it is hearing.

That's twelve pieces of information in the second or two that the music is playing, especially as many notes are played at the same time.

*Three Groups of Information*

But if the brain can recognize patterns and group things as it processes these patterns, it now only has three pieces of information to process (3 groups) rather than twelve individual pieces of sound. This is more efficient, time saving and less exhausting.

But music has more than just pitch and rhythm. Putting words to music brings even more complexity.

Pretend you didn't know how this song went (in the following diagram) and you were reading the words for the first time.

*Lyrics to Unfamiliar Songs*

Because English is your first language, you would recognize the words and it would be seen as ten pieces of information.

*Lyrics to Familiar Songs*

If you knew how the song went, you would group this phrase as one piece of information, leaving the rest of working memory and the brain space to process more information.

*Lyrics to Unfamiliar Songs in a Different Language*

If English was your second language, and you didn't know the song, your brain would interpret each individual character and it would be thirty-eight pieces of information. You can see how overwhelming that would be and until you start to know phrases and how the melody sounded, it would be exceedingly difficult to follow along.

It is the same with listening to music. The more we become familiar with it, the more our brain sees the grouping and then it can go from working memory to other parts of memory and be used in other ways.

When children hear the music for the first time, they don't know the words and they don't know the symbols and it can be overwhelming, but the more they listen to it, the more it can bring calm to an anxious and stressed brain.

Finding patterns, or grouping, allows the brain space and time to process the normal things it needs to. If we went to bed with static playing (where there is no pattern, just sound) we send our brain into overdrive trying to find the patterns which is overwhelming and exhausting.

Even if we were physically sleeping, it would not be restful or restorative sleep.

*Music has lots of patterns and gives the brain something to hold onto*

---

1. https://abcnews.go.com/Technology/story?id=97635

# Our Biggest Toxic Threat

H ow important is our auditory sound environment? How much attention should we pay to it?

Let's look back in time to see how things have changed.

*Born 1887*

This is my grandfather – Thomas Canning Hubbard. He was born in 1887 in South Australia. The world he was born into was vastly different to ours.

## Let's look at what his world might have looked like from an auditory point of view:

- No electricity

- No cars – horses/carts or walking for transport

- Many people were poor – no shoes. From a sensory and bone conduction perspective, this would have made a significant difference. More information would have been processed through the skeletal system because they were barefoot a lot.

- Played outside (children seen but not heard). Because of the lack of environmental noise and industry and high condensation of living areas had not settled in yet, there was birdsong and nature sounds, which they were heavily exposed to for a large part of the day.

- Listened to live music for entertainment or created their own music (for example with a harmonica or fiddle)

- Wooden toys

- No motors

- Noise levels would have been incredibly different to our day

- Long-distance travel was by ship or coach (on land) so no noise from airplanes or trains

Knowing what we know about outside nature sounds and birdsong you can see the difference between the stressors on their brains and auditory system and ours. Let's look a little further ahead in history.

*Born 1922*

This was my mother. She was born in 1922. Her clothing was sewn by hand by her mother and only the wealthy had cars, so there were only a few of them around. Let's think about the auditory environment in my Mother's day.

• Candlelight and lamps. There were no fluorescent lights or any light source that made a noise like our lights do.

• A few cars – but only for the wealthy so they walked everywhere or caught a tramcar into the city when she was in her twenties.

• No washing machines or kitchen appliances

• No refrigerator. They had an ice chest but no refrigerator with a motor.

• Toys for children were handmade and wooden. There was no plastic, noisy toys

• Played outside from the time they got home from school to the time they were to be home for dinner. They climbed trees and sat eating fresh fruit listening to all the sounds that nature offered

- No computers
- Entertainment – dancing to live music or listening to the radio at home
- No air conditioning or motorized fans
- No travelling in airplanes

Her auditory environment was noisier than her father's, but it was still relatively quiet when you think about today.

Let's roll forward to 1966.

*Born 1966*

I was born in 1966. The world had changed quite a bit since my mother was born. Cars were common, trains and air travel were also common and not just for the wealthy.

Let's look at other differences:

• Electricity was in every home, but lights were incandescent bulbs not fluorescents yet

• Cars were widely used so there was more traffic/road noise

• Sewing machines were common and we had some kitchen appliances

• We played outside after school. There was no social media or cell phones so we would usually play with neighborhood kids or have a friend over. We were outside climbing trees, playing in gardens, and enjoying nature sounds (birdsong)

• No computers or cell phones

• Entertainment – watching TV, boardgames, playing together as siblings or with friends – usually outside

• Television (although only black and white when I was young and then color later – in our house anyway).

• Motorized fans

• Travel in airplanes, trains, buses and more air traffic overhead. International travel was infrequent.

The world I grew up in was far noisier than my mother's time, although we still spent a significant amount of time outside playing. As a baby I didn't go lots of places, mostly home and to pick up siblings from school, so my auditory environment was quiet compared to my grandchildren's time.

Fast forward to 2018.

*Born 2018*

My granddaughter was born in 2018, vastly different from 1966 and a considerably noisier environment than the one I was born into. With the advancements in technology, it also increased the amount of noise in her everyday environment. Let's look at 2018:

- Electricity – Fluorescents
- High Traffic Noise
- Machines for Everything
- Play inside and at parks
- Noisy Toys (digital, plastic etc)
- Computers in every home and hand
- Spent a lot of time out and about in a noisy environment going to appointments etc
- Television

- Central air conditioning/heating
- Travel in airplanes, trains etc

Outside play was not every day for hours like it was when I was growing up and when it was outside, there were plenty of competing noises. Because she lives in an apartment complex, you don't hear birdsong very often or natural sounds like leaves crunching, trees rustling in the wind etc.

The auditory environment was much busier with noise both indoors and outdoors all the time. There was never a time, even when going to bed, when there was no sound.

My grandson was born into a COVID-19 environment in early 2021. Let's look at the world he was born into and the changes that had occurred from the time his sister was born, only 3 years earlier.

*Born 2021*

This was during an environment with lockdowns and full mask wearing during COVID-19. It was a stressful time for all involved and certainly a different world again to the one his sister was born into.

The world had all the same advancements in technology and subsequent noise that was around in 2018, but in 2021 everyone was locked inside, not able to go outside to hear what nature sounds existed.

He has spent his entire life so far mostly indoors, amidst the continual noise of the following:

- Fluorescent lights
- Constant computers going (Dad was now working from home)
- Phones (the only way to contact family through video apps)
- Refrigerator
- Microwave
- Airconditioning/heating
- Fans

Look at the types of sound we are talking about. Do you remember the Tomatis listening zones? Low level sounds discharge the central nervous system. That can be a good thing, but not when those sounds are constant and unrelenting and don't contain any patterns for the brain to hold onto.

We have become accustomed to this noise, and it is unlikely you are even aware that it exists now. Take a moment to listen around you. What sounds do you hear?

There is sound all around us and with the COVID lockdowns and being stuck inside, unless we make a conscious effort to intervene, there is no relief from the constant barrage of noise.

 This brings me to the title of this chapter. What is our greatest toxic threat? It is exactly what we have found ourselves in for the 18 months during a strict COVID environment – constant low level sound; "white noise" with no patterns in it. It is noise pollution!

With a brain that searches for and identifies patterns, our environment creates extra stress and ties the brain up with tasks that stop it from performing its normal processing successfully.

Remember also that our auditory system never shuts off, processing both through air conduction and bone conduction 24/7. COVID and all it has brought was stressful enough, but on top, we have been in an environment that is toxic to our system without even knowing.

It is an environment that puts extra stress on the brain and body (low level white noise) with no balance of energizing high frequency sounds coming in (higher tones like birdsong and nature sounds).

The result is that we have less patience, we are more physically tired, drained, and unable to perform tasks in the same productive way. All of this while trying to learn to work from home, managing different schedules in the same house, learning to homeschool, devoid of outside play and socialization. Are you starting to understand why COVID has been so difficult on so many levels?

Let's recap the reasons we have discussed so far for the prevalence of anxiety and depression increasing in our children and adolescents.

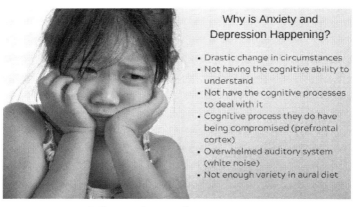

*Why Anxiety and Depression?*

•   Drastic change in circumstances that have required them to adapt very quickly

•   Not having the cognitive ability to understand what is happening and what a global viral threat is

•   Not having the cognitive processes to deal with it

- The cognitive processes that they did have were compromised due to the new circumstances we found ourselves in (prefrontal cortex)
- Overwhelmed auditory system (white noise)
- Not enough variety in the aural diet

## THE STORY OF JB

I was working with a client of mine a few years ago who had poor auditory processing skills. He was on the autism spectrum (was high functioning) and had sensory issues. I'll call him JB. It is the perfect example of how an auditory environment can be so overwhelming that it can cause the body and brain to shut down.

JB was 4 years old. He was a beautiful little boy with a loving family who just wanted him to be able to achieve whatever he was capable of. We were using sound therapy and other musical activities to work with his particular challenges.

While pleasant, JB could also be extremely stressful. Navigating the world of autism was a minefield and this family found challenges with his behavior and knowing what to do to help him. They were stressed and just wanted a bit of normality in their family.

They decided that it would be a good idea to just forget everything and spend some time together at a theme park. It was about a 3-hour drive away from where they lived so they figured they would make it a day trip and he would sleep on the way home.

The day began wonderfully. The line-up to get in wasn't too lengthy and before long they were inside, enjoying themselves.

JB seemed to like some of the slower rides they took him on, and it was all going to plan.

After a couple of hours, they noticed JB was getting tired. He was getting fussy and was hard to settle. They had expected that might happen so had brought a stroller for him to get into so they could push him around. After more time went by, his body started to slump, and he was quieter.

They thought he would just fall asleep in the stroller after a while. They didn't think anything of it, until they went to check he was out of the sun and noticed that he was drooling. While normal when he was younger, it was not something that JB did now.

He was more lethargic as time went on until he began looking pale and was not as responsive as usual. Their concern turned into panic, and they ended up in urgent care in the hospital.

After several hours and observation, he was much better, and they were eventually released and headed back home. So, what had happened to JB? Was it food poisoning? Was it sunstroke? Was he just ill?

Think about the challenges this child had. He didn't process sounds well and all sensory input that was coming into his body did not follow the normal channels for being recognized, processed, and responded to. His auditory and sensory challenges made normal things exceedingly difficult.

On this day, he had been thrust into an environment where there was more visual stimulus than normal, much more auditory input and with an auditory system that never shuts off, it became completely overwhelming. His body and brain would have been trying to process everything through both bone and air conduction and the result was catastrophic.

It wasn't a massive tantrum or meltdown of loud, epic proportions, it was just as alarming even though it was quiet and still. The brain will always protect itself and if it can't cope, it will start shutting things down.

Once JB was in the hospital (even though there are all sorts of sounds going on there) the auditory input was lessened enough for his body to regroup (over time) and start processing things again.

## Let's think about what he would have experienced at the theme park:

• Sounds of the rides (these can get extremely loud and when you have many of them going together, it can be overwhelming). They can also be unpredictable.

• People screaming

• Loud music playing as they went past each ride and booth

• Machines and engines

• People walking and chattering

• Fireworks and sound effects (at a show they went to)

The level of sound constantly entering his system proved to be totally overwhelming. It stressed his auditory system, his central nervous system, and his brain.

Sound can energize and makes us feel like dancing, but it also has the ability to make us feel tired, stressed, or worse, to shut down.

We need strategies in our toolkit to know how to cope with overwhelm, or better, to avoid it in the first place.

# Strategies to Build Aural Skills

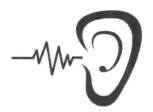

W hat can we do now to help our children? We have spoken a lot about the auditory side of things so what types of things can we do to help facilitate better aural skills to counteract some of the deficit they have been exposed to?

## STRATEGY #1: BE AWARE

Being aware of our auditory environment is essential if we want to see improvements. Taking an auditory audit and knowing what sounds energize and which drain is important.

There are sounds we must live with (computers, refrigerators, computers etc) so we need to make sure there is a balance of good sounds in our overall environment.

Here are some questions you can ask when assessing where you and your child are in your everyday lives, now that we are able to go outside, and some things have returned to normal:

• How much "white noise" is in your child's current environment?

• How many hours a day do they spend in that space?

• How much time is spent outside?

• Does your outside environment have naturally occurring nature sounds or is it limited to more urban, competing noise such as traffic sounds, overhead airplanes etc?

• How much music does your child listen to?

• Do I play active listening games with my child?

• How much speech does your child hear in their day? (Preferably live speech, not speaking over the television)

• Does your child say "huh" a lot when you ask them questions?

• Does your child follow through with instructions you give?

• Does your child sing songs?

• If your child sleeps with music or a noise machine, does the sounds they listen to have patterns (for example waves on a beach have patterns but static doesn't)

• Do I read books with my child?

- When I play music do I play it too loudly?

- Do I allow my child to be in sound environments where it is too noisy? (this could be concerts, events with fireworks, a place of work)

While you can never balance hour for hour with inside/outside, you can make a plan to take steps to counteract some of the toxic noise in your child's environment.

One thing to be aware of is the sound level around children. Their filtration systems are much more immature than ours and we need to protect their auditory system.

Never put headphones on a baby under 2 years old and never place headphones on a pregnant woman's belly.

Being more aware of what is happening is the first step to making improvements. It's like trying to lose weight. You gradually learn more about nutrition. The more you know the more harmful foods you cut out and the better you feel. It is a process and one where you will make better and better sound choices over time. The more aware you are, the more change you will eventually be able to bring about.

## STRATEGY #2: LISTEN

I know that sounds simple but active listening is a learned skill and one we hone over time. Hearing is passive and something we either have or don't (if we have a hearing loss).

Listening involves more auditory skills than its passive counterpart hearing, much in the same way that seeing takes more skills and brain focus (active) than just looking with the visual system (which is passive).

*Hearing vs Listening*

# Hearing

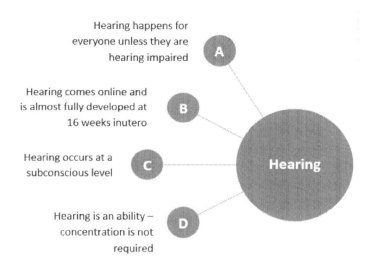

Hearing happens for everyone unless they are hearing impaired — A

Hearing comes online and is almost fully developed at 16 weeks inutero — B

Hearing occurs at a subconscious level — C

Hearing is an ability — concentration is not required — D

Copyright 2018 Diana F Cameron

*Hearing*

# Listening

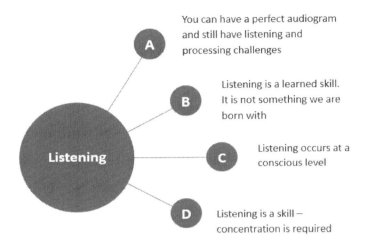

*Listening*

Developing the skill of listening will pay dividends not only in school for your children, but at home for when you give instructions or have conversations.

We have twelve essential auditory skills in total, but a big one needed for listening is auditory discrimination – being able to tell the difference and similarities between sounds.

There are a few steps involved in this skill which are:

1. Noticing
2. Comparing and

3. Distinguishing sounds

This is essential for language. For example, "three" and "free" are different but sound remarkably similar. If you didn't have good auditory discrimination, you would not be able to tell the difference. You might have two of the three elements, but that can still cause issues.

If you noticed that there were two words and you noticed that they were different and in comparing them could not distinguish HOW they were different, you might end up with a child that substitutes "free" for "three". We need all three elements working correctly to be able to hear, process and duplicate language.

**SUGGESTED ACTIVITIES:**

• I hear with my little ear something that sounds like (name a sound - for example a dog or something that you can hear). Alternatively, you can make a sound and get your child to guess it and/or copy it themselves

• Listen to the sound environment (especially outside but can be done inside) and isolate a sound. Ask your child if they can hear it too. This forces them to really attune to one specific sound within their sound environment amongst competing sounds

- Tap or clap syllables to words as you say them. For babies, tap on their bodies (it will be a listening exercise) but once they are 2 years or above, they should be able to start saying and clapping with you

- SOUND SCAVENGER HUNT: This is just what it sounds like. You make up a list of sounds that you can hear around your house (inside and/or outside) and your child finds them all and puts a tick beside them when they are found. For a younger child, you could tell them whether it is inside and outside and help them find it by giving obvious clues (you would be with them the whole time).

## SOUND SCAVENGER HUNT IDEAS:

Be mindful of the age of your child. The younger the child, the more immature their auditory filtration systems and skills are sounds are going to have to be more obvious.

INDOORS: Choose specific sounds that you may find in your home or outside. You might have a freezer that makes a sound, or music might be playing.

For older children, you can make things more difficult. They may have to really attune to a sound to find it. It might be muffled or very low. They may not even be aware of the sounds that are there if they have heard them a lot - for instance, the sound the microwave makes.

OUTDOORS: Once again, you can choose a specific sound that you know the child will hear.

Some suggestions may be:

- a dog barking
- wind in the trees (on a windy day)
- birds
- water (if you have a water feature in the garden)
- rain (if it is raining)

Another way of doing a scavenger hunt is to put a category of a sound rather than the sound itself. This is good for older children. For example:

- animal sounds
- water sounds
- man-made sounds
- sounds you make yourself
- sounds made with wood
- sounds made with a stone

This will really get them thinking about the sound properties of objects and ways to manipulate them to make sound. Think of some other ones, the possibilities are endless!

# STRATEGY#3: USE MUSIC

 Do you remember what Tomatis discovered? That sound can be a nutrient. It can either charge or discharge the central nervous system. Music is a wonderful way to not only support a stressed brain, but to increase our auditory skills at the same time.

You can use music to help calm or energize. Lullabies are soothing because they have certain characteristics that promote calm.

They are a universal language that has been a part of every culture for as long as we know. Recent research in September 2020[1] and additional studies done at the Music Lab[2] have shown that regardless of the language of the lullaby, children will respond to them because they have the following commonalities in the music and words:

- Simple lyrics often repeated
- Repeating melodies
- Rhyming phrases
- Usually in triple meter or 6/8 time giving them a swinging or rocking motion. This rhythmic sound and feeling mimics the movement of the baby in the womb and is familiar and soothing
- Simple intervals that are "soft" and easy on the ear

- Underlying theme of love
- Slower tempo
- Lower tones

 There are many lullabies that you can find to play to your child or you could try to create your own. Your child will find your voice much more soothing than something recorded (even if you think you can't sing) so just make it about them and make it up.

If you think you are going to teach your child to sing out of turn because you do, that is a myth. You will teach your child to love singing and it will be a bonding experience. You can also use music in other ways.

- Play music with high violin or flute sounds to give your child experience with processing different sounds.
- Use music with a livelier tempo to energize and dance around the room together
- Learn songs together and sing
- Use piggyback songs during your routines
- Sing or say names and clap the syllables to them

## PIGGYBACK SONGS

A piggyback song is simply using the melody of a song you already know and supplementing different words. For example, most people know "Row row row your boat, gently down the stream." Imagine singing the following words:

> Brush, brush brush your teeth,
> Get them nice and clean,
> Merrily merrily merrily merrily,
> Life is but a dream.

That is a piggyback song. You can use them for anything. They make chores seem shorter and it is an easier way for you to get young children to do mundane tasks while also strengthening their auditory and speech skills.

You can use them for anything – packing up toys, helping you cook, doing the washing, cleaning a room, washing walls, any repetitive task you can think of. They are simple and short, and kids will be singing with you in no time.

Getting your child to sing with you teaches them important auditory skills by hearing and processing different timing and rhythm (where the notes fall), pitch (whether the note is high, low, or in between), dynamics (loudness of the sound) and memory (having to remember the melody and the words).

All these skills are needed for speech so singing songs is a wonderful way to learn and strengthen language skills.

## MUSIC & DANCE

Putting music on and just dancing around the room is the perfect way to develop spatial awareness – another important auditory skill.

As you move around the room, the source of the sound remains the same. Your auditory system needs to work out where your body is in relation to the source of sound; an important auditory skill in keeping us safe.

This is another important skill that has been impacted by being inside all the time during COVID. Our children have not had opportunities to hear cars coming from different directions, children playing in a playground in front of them, behind and as they run past. They have not been to concerts, or even school where they hear students talking in various parts of the room. Their exposure has been limited and so we need ways to supplement.

Even though we are now back outside, and resuming our normal activities, there has been a long time without using these skills so now we need to catch up.

Kids love to move. You could do mirror dancing where you copy each other, or just move anyway that you want to. Use a variety of music so you can express yourself in diverse ways.

**Some examples of variety are:**

- Fast music

- Slow music

- Music that changes from fast to slow and back again

- Loud music (could be big movements)

- Quiet music (could be small movements or something like tiptoeing)

- Big music (with a full orchestra)

- Lighter music that might only have one or two instruments or an instrument and a vocalist

Think variety and get as much of it into their auditory diet as you can.

## STRATEGY #4: USING MUSIC TO TRAIN THE BRAIN TO RELAX

Another way to use music to calm the entire central nervous system and the brain to relax is to establish a daily routine where you just stop and either lie down or sit and just listen to a piece of music.

Consistency is the most important part of this. You also must be committed to just sitting and relaxing. Our brains have become so distracted and busy with our technology-driven lives that our brains and bodies have lost the art of relaxation.

Stress comes because a central nervous system just won't "let go". Have you ever had a remedial massage when you have had tight muscles? It is a painful experience. If you have a good massage therapist who knows anatomy, they know how to force the muscle to let go and relax. It is excruciating but the relief afterwards is undeniable.

Our bodies, when stressed, hold that stress. We hold it in our minds, in our muscles and in the very cells of our being. After the trauma of COVID and all it has meant in our lives, we need to retrain our brains and bodies to relax on cue.

The more you do these exercises, the quicker you will get into relaxation because you will have trained your body and brain to do it.

Simply choose some music that is soothing to you. It doesn't have to be a lullaby, but it does need to feel soothing. The important word there was FEEL. Different people react differently to music so choose something that when you hear it, you can see yourself on a beach somewhere with not a care in the world.

Put the music on, sit or lie down and for the duration of the song just try not to think. Don't analyze the music, don't construct a mental list of all the things you need to do when you get up, just sit, and let your mind wander.

At the start, for some people, this will be difficult. It won't feel comfortable. You may even feel agitated and like you need to get going and get things done. Those are all signs that you really need this kind of intervention, as simple as it is.

The more you do it (and it doesn't have to be the same piece of music each time – just something you find soothing) the quicker your mind and body will let go. You will find your body can learn to relax immediately. Just as your body knows what to do when you get into the driver's seat of a car, it can learn to wind down quickly when you start a routine that you do every day and practice with consistency.

That is one of the greatest gifts you can give your children and yourself. Relaxation is a learned skill, one that we can unlearn if our bodies and brains are constantly in a state of stress and anxiety. This is what I am seeing increasingly more since the pandemic. It is silent, you may not even notice that you or your children are stressed. When we live with chronic stress and anxiety, our bodies hold it, and tight muscles and poor sleep becomes the norm. If you do it for long enough your body and brain will be retrained into how to relax and reach that state of equilibrium.

Every day, one song (or more if you need it) just sit or lie down and just let your mind wander. If you find that difficult, this is something you can add to the exercise that may help.

# STRATEGY #5: MINDFUL BREATHING

We all breathe, or we wouldn't be alive, but mindful breathing is a way of centering us, forcing us to be in the moment and to calm our brains and bodies.

If you have trouble with the previous strategy, then adding this may help, especially if your mind keeps creating things to think about like tasks, lists etc.

Simply breath in and count slowly to four, then breathe out and count slowly for the same amount. Concentrate on each breath. Feel it come in, feel it go all the way in through your nose, down the back of your throat and into your lungs. Feel your body push it out. Be aware of the muscles that make that happen.

You don't have to continue counting once you are able to really focus on the breath coming in and going out. This will automatically start to lower your heart rate and help you relax.

For a child who has anxiety, mindful breathing can really help bring them back to the present. It also has a physical effect on the body, helping it to slow down in the same way a slower tempo does with a lullaby.

This can be done while listening to music or at any time and in any place. The brain can't be thinking of two things at once so by concentrating on the actual breath, you force it to stop its busyness and to focus on something soothing.

Young children can be taught to use this method at any time, whether they feel fine, stressed, angry or anxious.

**The proven benefits of daily mindful breathing are:**

- Reduce stress levels in the body
- Lower heart rate
- Lower blood pressure
- Improve diabetic symptoms
- Reduce depression
- Reduced stress
- Reduced anxiety
- Better manage chronic pain
- Better regulate the body's reaction to stress and fatigue
- Improved cognitive functions like memory, attention and focus
- Better emotional regulation

# STRATEGY #6: USE YOUR VOICE CREATIVELY

Using your voice creatively provides additional opportunities for your child to develop aural skills.

Often, we use the same type of voice simply because we are inside. We are not calling or yelling (hopefully not too much anyway) and so we don't get the variety we hear in a playground, or on a sports field. We haven't been able to sing in choirs or attend dance classes. All of these were important opportunities to practice aural skills where we heard diverse types of voices at different volumes.

With COVID, with being inside for an extended period, there are many vocal sounds, registers, and ranges that our children have missed.

To help counteract this lack of processing, we can use our voices in a variety of ways to counteract some of that diminishing skill.

There are several ways of doing this but here are some ideas:

- Vocal play

- Reading books

- Voice tracking – this is just what it sounds like. Just as you follow or track an object with your eyes, you do the same with your voice, following the movement of an object and making the sound match

- Rhyming words

**VOCAL PLAY**

Vocal play doesn't have to be organized or even prepared. Use your voice in silly ways, using variety and getting your child to copy you whenever possible. They will gain more skills if they do it with you than just listening. Make a game out of it and have fun. These sounds might include:

- High sounds
- Low sounds
- Growling sounds
- Loud sounds
- Quiet sounds
- Whispering
- Sounds gradually going up
- Sounds gradually going down
- Funny sounds made with nonsense syllables
- Made up words
- Animal sounds
- Imitating sounds you hear

You can also relate sounds to other things, adding a layer of complexity. For example, a big dog has a low bark. A small dog has a higher bark. Whatever you decide to do, have fun with it.

## READING BOOKS

Reading books can be so much more fun (and educational) if you use your voice in ways that are creative.

### Ideas might include:

• Using a different voice for different characters when they speak. Using a deep voice for men, a higher voice for women and for other characters, anything you like. Have fun with it and be as silly as you want.

• Vocalize events or things that happen in the book. For example, if a squeaky gate opens, a car goes up the hill or the wolf huffs and puffs a house, then create the sounds using your voice. This is a fantastic way to enhance the story and to build auditory skills at the same time.

• If there is a repeated phrase over and over as there is in many children's books, you might even make up a melody to go with it. Your child will be singing it for you after a few times hearing it.

## VOICE TRACKING

Following the shape of an object is the same concept as eye tracking. If you track something with your eyes, as it moves, your eyes move with it.

With voice tracking, your voice moves so the sound you make matches what you are visually seeing. Here are some ideas to use:

• You and your child take a scarf and move it from low to high, making a vocal slide (on any vowel sound) to match it. It would become a vocalization from low to high.

• Take a torch and shine it on the wall. As you move it create a vocal sound matching what you are seeing. This could be up and down, circles, a zig zag shape, or any other movement you choose to do.

• Use the torch at nighttime. Lie on your backs and make your stars (the torch) dance on the ceiling, while vocalizing.

• Match your torch movements to a song as you sing it. For example: If you sang Insy Wincy Spider it might look something like this:

Incy Wincy Spider
Climbed UUUUPPPPP the water spout (scarf or torch moves up as you do a vocal slide to match it)
Down came the rain (scarf or torch moves down on "down")
And wash the spider out (swish scarf or move torch from side to side)
Out came the sunshine and dried up all the rain (move scarf or torch in circles)

So Incy Wincy spider goes UUUPPPPP the spout again (move scarf or torch in the same way as the beginning with a vocal slide)

*Incy Wincy Spider Example*

## RHYMING WORDS

Kids love making up rhyming words and doing so helps them to notice the similarities and differences in language which is another important aural skill. Without it, we would not be able to match what we are hearing with what we produce and would mix up words.

The fun thing about it is rhyming words don't have to be real words. There are lots of possibilities and your child will have fun making things up.

Children start doing this typically around 3 years of age. Some can hear that a word is the same (like hat and mat) before that but to create rhyming words themselves out of a word you give them, they would typically need to be 3 – 4 years of age.

Start with something easy and that with lots of possibilities like:

• Hat

• Mat

• Rat

• Sat

• Cat

• Bat

- Fat

You can then move onto more difficult ones that don't have obvious answers. Things like:

- Elephant
- Lion
- Tiger

You can put any consonant in front of a word to make a rhyming word. For example:

Elephant | Pelephant | Selephant

Lion Tion | Slion | Bion

Try using their name and rhyming with that:

Diana | Biana | Triana | Sliana

As I said, things don't have to make sense and usually the sillier the better kids like it. Have fun with it and see if you can construct a story out of the silly words that you have made.

1.  Bainbridge, C.M., Bertolo, M., Youngers, J. et al. Infants relax in response to unfamiliar foreign lullabies. Nat Hum Behav 5, 256–264 (2021). https://doi.org/10.1038/s41562-020-00963-z

2. https://www.themusiclab.org/

# Another Issue with Developmental Skills in a COVID Environment

A big sensory system that has been impacted for every child because of our COVID environment is the vestibular system.

The vestibular system is commander and chief of all sensory input and when that isn't working correctly, children end up with sensory issues. This could manifest in many ways from difficulty in learning, sensory sensitivities, being agitated and anxious or poor motor skills and balance just to name a few.

Imagine you are at a busy train station. People are everywhere. Some are talking, some yelling, there is noise all around. A train is coming, and the announcer says, "Sydney train approaching." There is a chance that you will hear correctly, but you might misinterpret the statement, or worse, miss it altogether.

Instead of hearing "Sydney train approach" your brain hears "Cindy is a cockroach." It doesn't make sense, and your brain goes into overdrive, concentrating, trying to figure out what was said.

When our brain interprets things correctly, it is easy to follow through with a response or action. But when it misinterprets something, it stops performing its normal function and concentrates on solving the puzzle at hand.

The same is true with our vestibular system. When it doesn't interpret information correctly, the same confusion happens.

When everything is working as it should, this system works like an air traffic controller. All the information that enters our brain through our various senses hits the vestibular system first and its job is to direct the information to the correct parts of the brain.

> *"A well working vestibular system means a better organized brain. A better organized brain means less stress and learning comes more easily."*
> Diana F Cameron

Problems occur when the controller misinterprets information or is confused about where to send the information. Sometimes it may even slow down, or snooze, or miss something completely.

A vestibular system that is not functioning correctly will affect how we learn and our behavior. Your child's vestibular system might even be like Wi-Fi, continually dropping out, giving intermittent signals leaving your child to guess what goes in between. When this happens, your child might zone out.

Children are sensory creatures. They interpret the world through all their senses. The vestibular system, although commander and chief, integrates with the other sensory systems to help information come together seamlessly in split second timing.

It works with touch so when your child touches something hot, it provides the avenue for the quick retrieving movement, so they are not burned.

It integrates with the auditory system so if your child was riding their bike and heard an out-of-control car coming straight for them, they could move out of the way.

It works with the visual system to help stabilize our eyes during movements. If this didn't happen, it would be like those home movies you see where the world moves quickly up and down as someone is walking around.

Reading books would be impossible because the words would move on the page as your head moved from side to side while reading.

If our vestibular and visual systems give us contradictory information, then children can experience travel sickness.

This integration and working together seamlessly relies on the vestibular system gathering, interpreting, and sending information to the right parts of the brain for further integration.

When this system has so much to do with movement is it any wonder that children learn naturally in this way? Children want to move. They like to rock, spin, jump and roll. There is a reason that music and movement go together for young children. Movement is how they interpret the world around them and learn.

By moving, they stimulate this system and that gives them energy.

Have you ever started falling asleep, trying to do work, and shaken your head to make yourself more alert so you could concentrate better? That movement is stimulating the vestibular system to help you wake up.

The vestibular system also has to do with balance. Balance is achieved more easily when we are moving than when we are still.

In the military, soldiers who need to stand still for extended periods of time will wiggle their toes. This can't be seen by anyone, but by stimulating the vestibular system in this way, it helps to maintain balance.

Think about learning to ride a bike. It is much easier to balance on the bicycle when it is moving fast than when it is moving slowly.

Have you ever wondered why you get so tired on a long-haul flight? Part of the reason is to do with your vestibular system not being active. You will be less fatigued if you get up and walk around every now and then instead of just sitting the whole time.

Sitting still for some children seems impossible; they need to move. If their vestibular system is not working correctly, sitting still for something like schoolwork or story time is going to be much more difficult than moving around while listening.

Standing still or sitting still requires the highest level of balance. If the vestibular system is compromised, then other parts of the brain need to stop doing their job and try and work on keeping upright.

The surface of the brain is called the cerebral cortex. Although it is less than half a centimeter (0.2 of an inch) thick, it is critical in our ability to move, to understand what we see, and what we hear and think.

It is a complex process of:

- making decisions
- learning

- remembering, and

- planning.

So, if it is busy just trying to work out which way is up, it is not free to process all these other functions effectively, and some of them are compromised. Then we can see delays and deficits in learning and behavior.

The vestibular system is a set of sensors near the middle ear that are sensitive to where your head is in space. It relies on gravity to tell your brain where your body is.

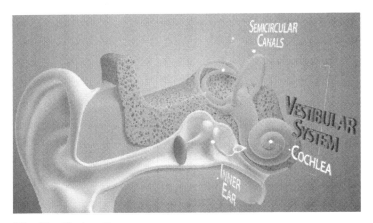

*The Vestibular System*

The vestibular system helps to protect our body and brain. When a baby learns to walk, their developing sense of balance protects the head by having them fall backwards onto their bottom rather than forwards onto their face. This is the vestibular system at work.

When we have learned how to walk and run, if we trip or fall, our first instinct is to put our hand out to stop ourselves from falling. That is also driven by the vestibular system spurring us into action to protect the body and brain. Within fractions of a second the brain puts this motor system into action to prevent us from experiencing serious damage.

Think back to our COVID environment. We were not in a position where children could do all those big body movements that they need for the vestibular system to learn how to process sensory information. They were confined indoors, doing more fine motor activities, or using their visual system more as their screen time increased because of online school, television, video apps to socialize with friends and social media.

## VESTIBULAR SEEKING

What if our child's vestibular system doesn't take in enough information? What if your child was like a big cup and the drops of sensory input never filled that cup? You would have a child that needed to move all the time. The vestibular system and brain would seek after the types of activities that gave them more stimulation, and with some children, they never seem to want to stop.

This is because their system is in overdrive trying to satisfy the need for sensory input.

## For these children, you might see behaviors like:

- Unable to sit still

- Need to be constantly moving

- Extremely impulsive

- Running everywhere instead of walking

- Babies may hate tummy time as it is not enough movement

- Take unsafe risks (like jumping from high things, constantly climbing etc. These are children that seem to have no fear and just act)

- Love being upside down, or hanging off something

- Seem to be on full throttle all the time, especially during movement activities

- May have memory issues

- Love to be hugged extremely tightly

*Vestibular Seeking*

Children who are vestibular seeking will crave continual, increased movement, regardless of how much they get. They will never seem satisfied.

## VESTIBULAR AVOIDING

So, what if your child's vestibular system takes in too much information? When this happens, they will avoid movement. Think of your child as a tiny cup and each drop of sensory information comes in. It doesn't take long for the cup to be full and overflowing.

*Vestibular Avoiding*

**For these children you may see the following behaviors:**

- Won't like sports
- Won't like swinging
- Won't like spinning
- Won't like roller coasters
- Won't like hanging upside down on monkey bars
- Won't like being turned upside down
- May not like to be picked up
- They may appear weak (floppy or slouchy)

- May not like tummy time (because it is too much sensory input)
- May have difficulty with coordination
- May have difficulty with visual activities (tracking and focusing)
- They might avoid stairs or hold on with both hands to the railing
- May be fearful of elevators
- They may appear stubborn (when it is fear driving the behavior because the movement is too much for them)
- May have anxiety
- May have memory issues

A well working vestibular system means a better organized brain. A better organized brain means less stress and learning comes more easily.

So, children need to move their whole bodies, and lots of it. Movement is key to a happy healthy child.

Are you starting to see the mounting problems that our children are now facing post COVID?

The normal movements during play like running, riding bikes, rolling, jumping, playing on playground equipment, swimming, dancing, and sports have all been stopped. Being indoors has made it impossible for the normal avenue of learning to occur. Their ability to learn normal concepts in a normal way has been restricted during

COVID. This has an impact on learning. Not just movement but all types of learning.

Remember we said that sitting still and focusing takes the highest form of balance? Children learn better balance through the integration of the vestibular system with other sensory systems through all the big movements mentioned.

During COVID, and especially lockdowns, we were expecting our children to sit and focus in an environment that was already strained because of restrictions, with a prefrontal cortex not operating efficiently because of stress and no avenue to release that anxiety and built-up stress through movement (which would be normal channel for children to "blow off steam".

Add to that the additional stress of no socialization which children crave and we have a recipe for disaster.

Having had to endure those conditions for so long is it any wonder our children have emerged with higher levels of anxiety, depression, sensory issues, and subsequent learning difficulties?

This also impacts directly on behavior with a decreased ability to control emotions, self-regulate, less patience and poor decision making.

## THE VESTIBULAR SYSTEM IMPACTS DIRECTLY ON BEHAVIOR

I have always said that behavior is a language. Our child's behavior is a window into what is going on in the brain. The brain is responsible for processing information from all inputs and sending the information to the correct areas so skills can be put into practice.

We have spoken about the auditory system, (and skeletal system), our vestibular system and other senses and how they work together to take in information, so your brain has the information needed to perform its complex tasks.

While they each have a specific role to play, they are so interwoven that in split second timing, our bodies respond.

Your child walks into a room. Their eyes tell them where they are, their ears tell them what is happening around them and their vestibular system tells them if they are still, moving, standing, or sitting. This information is constantly and seamlessly updated so they can respond physically when necessary.

In a brain that doesn't have a well-organized vestibular system, input may be slow to where it needs to get to, or information may be relayed intermittently. Information might be missed altogether but the pace of everything going on around them still moves at the same speed.

They get more overwhelmed with time, and it isn't long before that overwhelm shows in behavior.

Three things relating to behavior that are directly impacted by a sluggish or disorganized vestibular system are:

1. Arousal
2. Motor systems and
3. Language

# Strategies to Strengthen the Vestibular System

W e have discussed why the vestibular system is so important. The first thing any parent needs to do is work out whether their child is vestibular seeking or vestibular avoiding. Here are some characteristics that may help you figure that out. Children don't have to display all the characteristics below, but you will know if you are seeing a pattern of one category or the other.

## Your child may be vestibular seeking if they:

• love movement and want more all the time

• like being on the ground on their stomach on the floor

• seem to be constantly moving and find it hard to sit still and focus

• love spinning or other fast, intense movements and never appear dizzy

• always jumping on furniture, spinning on swivel chairs, or hanging in upside down positions

• tend to run, jump, or hop everywhere instead of walking

• tend to rock their body or shake their head or shake their leg while sitting still

• love sudden, quick movements like going over a hump on their bike, having an airplane move in a storm or going over big bumps in the car

If they are **vestibular seeking**, it means they are hyposensitive to movement and are under-responsive. They will crave big movements and lots of them. Nothing will seem uncomfortable. These are the kids you see Dad's flying through the air, and they are laughing and loving every minute of it.

## Your child may be vestibular avoiding if they:

- cling to you constantly

- dislike elevators or escalators and may even sit down when using them

- dislike climbing ladders and can be fearful of stairs or ground that is uneven (like soft sand at the beach)

- are fearful of jumping or other things that cause their feet to leave the ground

- dislike swings, trampolines, slides or spinning playground equipment

- as a baby dislikes bouncers and swings

- lose their balance easily and appear clumsy

- have difficulty balancing on one foot (if you suspect this, try with their eyes closed which will be more difficult for them if they are vestibular avoiding)

- get startled if they are not in control of their own movement (for example someone else moving them when they don't expect it)

- hate being upside down or any movement that tilts the head. They hate having their hair washed over a sink

- are afraid of heights, even something that you may consider small like a curb

- are constantly in fear of falling (even if there is no risk of falling)

- prefer sitting still activities like sitting on the ground playing with cars or blocks

- prefers minimal movement and where they are in total control of that movement

Children who are **vestibular avoiding** are <u>hypersensitive to movement</u> and <u>over-responsive</u>. Even the slightest motion can seem too much for them and they will start to cry because they are uncomfortable. These are the kids that don't like to be rocked, or to swing or even things like going in an elevator might set them off.

Knowing your child and what their boundaries are is vitally important to work within the bounds of what is tolerable. Be guided by them by watching their reactions. It does no good to push a child past overwhelm as they will just associate movement with something unpleasant which impacts on the original issue.

It doesn't matter which end of the spectrum they are on (seeking or avoiding), they need help strengthening this system. Choose from the appropriate list of activities depending on your child's needs.

# Suggested Activities to Build a Stronger Vestibular System

## CALMING VESTIBULAR ACTIVITIES FOR THOSE WHO ARE VESTIBULAR AVOIDING

1. Rocking back and forth in a rocking chair (movements may need to be smaller - be guided by your child's reaction)

2. Slow marching in a straight line.

3. Inverting the head by hanging upside down either on play equipment or across a bed (some children find this calming; other children dislike this position)

4. Slow rocking sitting on a therapy ball.

5. Three ways of Rocking

6. Tuck and Rock – lay on the floor on your back, bring your knees to the chest and wrap arms/hands around knees so body is in a ball shape. Rock back and forth slowly on your back.

7. Rocking back and forth on all fours on the floor.

8. Rocking in a hammock

9. Swaying or slowly dancing to music

10. Yoga (especially inversion poses)

11. Sitting on a gliding chair or couch

12. Riding a rocking horse

13. Swinging in a blanket swing (have child lay in blanket and have two adults each hold an end and lift to swing back and forth)

## VESTIBULAR STIMULATION FOR THOSE WHO ARE VESTIBULAR SEEKING

1. Rocking in a hammock

2. Three ways of rocking

3. Linear movements

4. Vertical movements

5. Rotary movements

6. Upside down movements

7. Horizontal movements

8. Experiencing an unstable base of support (like walking on uneven ground, soft sand on the beach, wobbly bridges)

9. Starts and stops in motion

10. Changes in direction

11. Changes in speed

12. Spinning in large circles on a tire swing **(Caution Below)**

13. Skipping

14. Galloping

15. Running

16. Somersault

17. Cartwheels

18. Jumping rope

19. Playing leapfrog

20. Moving across monkey bar

21. Riding a seesaw

22. Riding a merry-go-round

23. Standing upside down with feet up against wall

24. Climbing up the ladder and then sliding down slides

25. Jumping

26. Riding a bike/scooter

27. Riding rollerblades/roller skates

28. Riding push toys/bikes/scooters down a hill

29. Swinging - either sitting or standing

30. Having frequent breaks will be important, especially in environments where lots of sitting is required, like school

31. Using chewing to calm. Chewing is a way to stimulate the vestibular system without moving around so chewing gum is a great way to help calm a vestibular seeking child in school or where they need to sit for an extended period of time.

## SPINNING CAUTION

For vestibular seeking children they will spin and spin and never get dizzy. This can be an issue because there comes a point where the vestibular system will shut down from over stimulation. These children will spin at a fast rate continuously without stopping because spinning is the most intense form of vestibular input.

If the vestibular system shuts down, the child will become extremely nauseous, even to the point of vomiting. This may not be seen immediately but can present later and could last anywhere from a few hours to a couple of days (think about something like severe vertigo).

It doesn't mean you can't let them spin but limit the time and help them to spin 10 seconds one way, then stop them and get them to go the other way for 10 seconds. Doing this repeatedly will allow them to spin but limit the chances of vestibular overload and shut down.

# Three Way Rocking

T his is going to be the best thing to have in your parent toolkit. This is a method I have devised as a result of my experience and knowledge of the vestibular system, sound therapy and watching children 0 - 6 for the past three decades.

I have taught this to every parent who walks through my door because it is the easiest way I know to gently calm down the central nervous system and brain in stages, while supporting that system, even for vestibular avoiding children.

 I have seen children who suffer from night terrors that normally last for well over three hours, be able to calm in fifteen minutes after parents have used this method over time. I have seen children in complete overwhelm gradually be comforted as we do this activity.

It works, and is great to use for any situation, whether a child is calm or upset.

## Vestibular System Anatomy

Before we get into it, let's learn a little more about what the vestibular system is anatomically so you understand why this works. I promise I won't get all technical and scientific, but it is important you understand what we are trying to achieve when doing the three ways of rocking.

We mentioned before that the vestibular system was a set of sensors in the middle ear that were sensitive to where our head was in space. It detects three important things:

- motion
- head position
- spatial orientation

These sensors are made up of three semi-circular canals which are continuous with the cochlea. These are called the vestibular labyrinth. Each canal is situated in a plane in which the head can rotate. Each of the canals can detect one of the following head movements:

- nodding up and down
- shaking from side to side
- tilting left or right

Inside these canals is a system of fluid and hair cells. As the fluid flows over the tiny hairs, they move, sending signals to the brain which then interprets which way the head is moving.

Each semicircular canal is stimulated in a gentle and supporting way when we do three ways of rocking. These will be:

- Rocking front to back (otherwise known as embryonic rocking)
- Rocking side to side
- Rocking in a circular, rotational movement

Look at all movements from your child's point of view. For example, if you have them in your lap facing the same direction as you, and you rock side to side, that would be different if they were across your lap (which would be front to back for them when you rocked sideways).

You don't have to remain in the same position (if your child gets restless) but make sure you are getting in all three directions during the song.

## Directions:

1. Choose a song that is calming and has a beat that you can rock to that is slow. You don't want to rock quickly you want this to be slow and controlled.

2. Choose one way (it doesn't matter which direction you do first) and rock in that direction for a portion of the song. You want to give the brain time to detect the movement and feel that movement for a period before moving to the next one. You don't want to move too quickly through the stages.

3. After you have done one way for a while, change to the next direction

4. Make sure you have included all three directions of rocking during the song or songs

5. You can repeat as often as you need to either during the day or night, or in a row if you wish to rock for more than one song.

Rocking in this way gradually brings the brain and central nervous system down in stages. It supports the vestibular system but is also calming and systematic.

Rocking creates a bonding experience and brings a sense of security.

# Suggested Adaptions:

## For vestibular seeking children:

• hold them more tightly or if they need it, wrap them in a blanket like a cocoon. The extra pressure on their skin will give their vestibular system more input which they will find more tolerable

• make the rocking movements larger. The movement still needs to be controlled, smooth and slow, but making the movements larger will give them that greater input

## For vestibular avoiding children:

• hold them less tightly. If you have a child that doesn't like to be touched or needs to be in control of the movement themselves, have them sit on the floor next to you and hold a doll or stuffed animal and copy you

• make the rocking movements much smaller. The smaller the movement, the less vestibular input they are getting so it won't be overwhelming for them. This is a wonderful way to strengthen the vestibular system in a very gentle calming way, but movements might need to be small to begin with

## For any child:

• try hammocking. If rocking is new to your child, you may want to begin by hammocking. Simple lay out a blanket and get them to lie on it. You and another adult get at each end and swing them in the blanket.

Remember, small movements for those that are avoiding input and larger swings for those that are seeking more input.

# That's a Wrap!

L et's put all this together and just summarize what we have learned about COVID-19, our subsequent circumstances and what that has meant for our children.

COVID-19 brought about a drastic change in our circumstances. It meant living for extended periods inside, devoid of normal activities and socialization.

For children, who have limited understanding of abstract concepts and can't understand what a viral health threat is, they also lack the necessary cognitive skills to comprehend the changes to their situation.

Additionally, the cognitive abilities they do have (executive functions governed by the prefrontal cortex) were compromised due to the prolonged stressful conditions of isolation. This produced fear and uncertainty, again without having the necessary skills to understand or rectify their circumstances.

This has produced ongoing anxiety, fear, and depression.

Other normal child development processes have also suffered. The cancellation of normal childhood activities meant they did not get to hear and process normal sounds in outdoor environments and were subject to an increased amount of toxic noise inside. This put added stress on their bodies and brains while trying to deal with these sounds which resulted in building pressure on the central nervous system.

Without the opportunity to hear and process a variety of sounds in all registers, the acquisition of speech may have been affected along with creativity, alertness, and the ability to focus.

Without running, playing, and participating in large body movements for extended periods of time, the vestibular system may have become compromised resulting in an inability to interpret sensory input effectively.

The final result, now that we are emerging from isolation and resuming normal activities, is a generation of children who are anxious, depressed, fearful and lacking in some of the developmental skills needed to function and perform everyday tasks.

We have pulled them from home schooling, put them back into the classrooms and are now seeing more behavioral issues, focus and attention difficulties and learning delays.

We are now seeing a large population of children who need intervention. Their behavior needs to be seen for what it is - a cry for help and a display that things in the brain are disorganized and not processing information as it should.

Our children are anxious and stressed. For many of them the pandemic is not over but just beginning. Many are unable to recognize what is happening or powerless to articulate their needs.

We need to be observant, patient, caring and kind and provide them with the support and intervention necessary to get them back to a place of equilibrium and calm.

We are facing a silent pandemic; one that I believe we will not know the true cost of for many years.

Just as all those in the front lines were heroes during the worst of it, now parents and caregivers get to be the heroes of their own story as they help their children navigate the aftermath and lead them back to a place of healing and calm.

# The SILENT Pandemic After COVID-19

What You Won't Notice and What Your Children Can't Tell You

### Less Toxic Noise

Try to minimize your exposure to low level toxic noise

### More Time in Nature

Spend as much time in natural sounds and nature as possible

### 3 Way Rocking

Utilize rocking 3 ways to calm the brain and the central nervous system

### More Music

Listen to more music with patterns to give the brain something to hold onto

### Regular Relaxing

Take a couple of moments each day to stop, relax and listen to some music

### More Connection

Purposefully connecting with friends and family

# About the Author

Diana F Cameron has a Grad Dip in Education and a BA(Mus. Diana's career has spanned over three decades and has seen her combine her love of early childhood, learning differences, music and neuroscience.

She has two children (both married) and two grandchildren and she currently lives in Queensland, Australia.

Diana loves to compose music, write children's books, and do graphite drawings but most of all, she loves igniting the imaginations of children through her stories and educating parents and early childhood professionals about the role sound plays in every facet of learning.

# Also By Diana F Cameron

This book is also available as a course. It consists of short videos, text lessons, quizzes, downloads and a workbook to guide you through.

If you are interested in doing the course, because you have purchased the book you can have a 50% off voucher. Please use **PCH50OFF** to obtain your discount.

You will find the course here with my other available courses: **www.dianafcameron.com/courses**

Please see my **author page** to keep up to date with my latest releases

**www.amazon.com/author/dianafcameron**

Made in United States
Orlando, FL
24 October 2022

23785467R00080